A Path to the Sea

A Path to the Sea

Liliana Ursu

Translated by Liliana Ursu,

Adam J. Sorkin and Tess Gallagher

Pleasure Boat Studio: A Literary Press

Romanian originals © 2011 by Liliana Ursu (author)
English translations © 2011 by Liliana Ursu, Adam J. Sorkin, and
Tess Gallagher (translators)
ISBN 978-1-929355-75-4
Library of Congress Control Number: 2011924020

The cover painting is by Irish painter Josie Gray and is entitled "Golden
Alcove to the Sea."

This publication was supported in part by a generous grant from the
Romanian Cultural Institute, Bucharest.

Pleasure Boat Studio books are available through the following:

SPD (Small Press Distribution) Tel. 800-869-7553, Fax 510-524-0852
Partners/West Tel. 425-227-8486, Fax 425-204-2448
Baker & Taylor 800-775-1100, Fax 800-775-7480
Ingram Tel 615-793-5000, Fax 615-287-5429
Amazon.com and **bn.com**

and through

PLEASURE BOAT STUDIO: A LITERARY PRESS
www.pleasureboatstudio.com
201 West 89th Street
New York, NY 10024
Contact Jack Estes
Fax; 888-810-5308
Email: pleasboat@nyc.rr.com

For Andreea and Mihnea

Contents

Acknowledgments

Acknowledgments are due to the editors and publishers of the following publications where a number of these poems first appeared, sometimes in slightly different versions: *Absinthe, American Poetry Review, Artful Dodge, The Baltimore Review, Blackbird, Connotation Press, Crazyhorse, The Cortland Review, The Fourth River, Harpur Palate, The Hurricane Review, Image, The Kenyon Review, Lifeboat, The Massachusetts Review, Natural Bridge, Notre Dame Review, Orient Express, Perigee, Poetry International, Poetry London, The Poetry Miscellany, Poetry Wales, Rattle, Runes, The Salt River Review, Seattle Review, Seneca Review, Southern Humanities Review, Storie—All Write, Turnrow, Two Lines, Vallum,* and *World Literature Today.*

Liliana Ursu expresses thanks to the Fulbright Scholar Program, Penn State University, the Stadler Center for Poetry, Bucknell University and the Baltic Center for Writers and Translators for support during her stays in America and in Sweden during which much work was accomplished toward this book.

Adam J. Sorkin wishes to express gratitude to the Penn State University College, Penn State Brandywine, and the Institute for the Arts and Humanities for their support of his work on this book.

Pleasure Boat Studios, Liliana Ursu, Adam J. Sorkin, and Tess Gallagher note with gratitude the generous support of the Romanian Cultural Institute, Bucharest, under The Translation and Publication Support Programme.

Translator's Note

Tess Gallagher

"Like a ring of fire around fire," Liliana Ursu ends her poem, an image that also conveys the intensity of this book.

Translating these amazing poems was like translating lightning. They left me singed and stricken but lifted by their illuminations, their sudden, piercing power. Co-existing with Ursu's magical binding of the broken world with "word-shadow" is her close, wide child's eye fixed tenderly on wild strawberries, on the bird's egg fallen from its forest nest. She knows to leave the wasp's sting in us, allowing us "great pain / after great love."

Characteristic of her poems is the sword's dangerous whistle through air at the ends. "We take their heads!" she used to cry gleefully after we'd give joint readings together during travels for *The Sky Behind The Forest*, the first book on which Adam Sorkin and I worked with her. Indeed, there is a way her endings often disorient, and the reader feels slapped awake, put beyond reason, which is one of the things I have always loved about poetry in general. It is Ursu's special talent to carry us out of rational mind and into states of being which delight or cast us down to earth with such force we must recalibrate our stance entirely.

Ursu combines brilliant force of image with her ability to connect beloved elements of her Romanian homeland, her birthplace in Sibiu and her life in Bucharest, to her American sojourns in Pennsylvania and Kentucky, where she taught for periods. The silken web she weaves between continents, between her literature and ours, between her country's suffering under Ceaușescu and abutting her experience of American abundance and freedom, has much to teach us. She is a kindly guest as she takes on the blessings of travel in America, but she also lets us glimpse a certain spiritual dearth, for this is her strongest offering, that we sense in her a very deep and abiding religious center that nourishes all she sees and gives. One sits with her in the presence of icons and in the sanctuary of monasteries with those who have dedicated their lives in pursuit of spiritual knowledge and service. Although these are likely not our emblems, we enter authentically these alcoves of sanctuary and their extensions of belief through Ursu's straightforward reliance.

For a mostly secular literature such as our own, this is a rare gift offered without irony or judgment, and one whose bounty is available to us surprisingly without our having undertaken the adherences of this author. It is as if we inhale some rare and deliciously saving perfume whose essence mysteriously extends our notion of what a soul is and what it requires when challenged to stand naked and humble before life's extremities.

Abbey Cottage
Ballindoon
Co. Sligo

1.

Celebration in the Season of Nettles

It's Not a Good Time for Poets

The despair of my open hand
at the corner of my lips—
the tremor of my voice when I ask
in the Cibin market in Sibiu
for a kilo of cherries—these
are the fierce masks behind which I preserve myself
during days when another poet advises:
"Transform yourself into
something else, even a dragon. Forget
for a while you're a poet. It won't do
you any good. Can even
destroy you."

And I—who stubbornly continue to write poems,
to cull, to retrieve my youth
from photographs—gather lavender, stalk
by stalk, and spread it on my dead father's desk.
As if life were just going on,
comforting and gentle, imaginable.

As if my flesh were, yes,
what it is: a fountain of stars.

Celebration in the Season of Nettles

I haven't written any poems.
Not about the tribe of nettles and their uses,
nor about the cherry blossoms.
Winter felt endless
and my skittery sleep, like a startled rabbit
pursued by too many hunters, shook the dark.

There's little news:
the daffodils herald a fanfare of gold
in the monastery garden, and
Cati's old aunt was picked up by the wind
while hanging her patched blouses in the yard.
She's all right now.
She reads her favorite psalms in the glow
of her small table lamp, its backlit shade
a collage of half-century-old news clippings,
her photograph at twenty
when she was crowned *Miss Romania*.

Another Saturday night and fireworks sparkle like a tiara
in the quiet March sky. Who knows
what the guests at the Marriott might be celebrating?
As for me: my first poem
after an interminable winter.

Strolling Between Millennia

The young man proceeds serenely through the crowd
carrying a black violin case.

He strolls along the busy street,
a fair-haired young man in blue jeans and
leather jacket, as if he had appeared
out of the clear sky above a mountain
and not from the vertical abyss
of a ten-story apartment building.

The light sparkles shyly
on faces, on the brazen lindens,
on the miniature cross around the neck of a little boy
ripping crumbs from a heel of bread
to scatter for the birds.

From one window a Bach concerto,
from another the voice of the TV
reporting fresh bombardments
somewhere in the world.

The young man proceeds serenely through the crowd
carrying a black violin case.
This is how I imagine
an angel would pass among mortals.

He enters the apartment building, rises
to the sunny terrace on the roof above the tenth floor.
Among white linens drying on a red plastic clothesline,
he expertly clicks open the black case; how calmly
he assembles
the high-powered rifle.

Once Upon a Time in Venice

I dreamed I was in Venice.
I was twenty
and lightning was my brother.

On my scarf a hand from the sky
had painted curious signs.
My hair smelled of tangerines,
my breasts of almost ripe lemons.
I was living in a small hotel,
its name erased by thick fog.

At dawn, I'd wait for you on the embankment.
You were the merchant of pearls and myrrh.
Your lips had the taste of apples stored in hay,
your cheeks, the salt of tears mixed
with harbors and open seas.

You always arrived in May
after a year or two of absence, or three.
I always asked you the same thing:
"Where have you been these last two hours?"

The gondola on which you used to ferry me
was heaped with azaleas and freesias, alive with red
and blue birds; our bodies were drunk on love,
on the supreme sensuality of the stars.

You never spoke,
letting your voyages take the place of speech,
and even sometimes of life.

Whenever you sailed away, I'd go back
to my small Venetian room. I played chess
by myself, painted delicate scarves
with more and more complicated runes,
coordinates and alignments of the planets
calculated to bind us together again.

And every evening, in my small stove
of glazed white tiles, I burned
those long silk letters.

In the House where Hyacinths

bloom a second time, the snow
can no longer be heard against the window.
Nor the laughter of the mad king.

Olive trees are in flower in the Elysian Fields.
My silver hairpin
adorns other coils, the sheen
of other years.

Winter Impressions

At the wall licked clean by the snow's assiduous tongue
the soldier's tall boots stand sentry.
He himself has retreated into the Radio Building to get warm.
An unremarkable winter scene,
not in the least worthy of some modern Breughel's eye.

Nevertheless, here at the boundary between the necessary
and the useless, a cat has had her kittens
in one of the soldier's boots.
The small shapes—new eyes
still blind to winter, to the absence
around them—turn small pink mouths
toward the hot belly of the present.

The skein of life unwinds. Spatters of milk
flicked from their white whiskers
melt the ice, drop
by drop.

Return to Sibiu

After a year of absence
I find my house strewn with feathers.

From the paintings, what first disappeared
was the sea.
Only a fish's gasping mouth remained alive,
bubbling words.

Moon rays curled obediently
in my coffee cup
and an invisible bird measured invisible time
inside a clock where she'd built her nest.

"Georg," she whispered.
"Philipp," the echo sang back.
"Telemann," I say aloud
while the record is spinning
and violin strings
accompany your body
a world away.

Like an unseen orchestra:

> *Presto*, say your fingers
> *Corsicana*, answer my fingers
> *Allegrezza*, say your eyes
> *Scherzo*, answer mine
> *Gigue*, say your patent-leather shoes
> *Polacca*, answers my white dress
> *Menuet*, answer our bodies, dancing in a ring
>> on the perfect Street of the Bards . . .

The Silver of Our Moment

Ignorant, the snail crosses both good and evil,
the sensations of each, as it caresses earth,
sometimes warm and tempting, sometimes
cold, devoid of answers.
Its journeys embroider silver lace
on truths, half truths and lies—
a work of art
by such a slow, insignificant creature,
easily crushed
by the wickedness of the powerful,
by negligence or accident.

I watch it advance with the same sweet patience
it uses to carry itself
along blades of grass, the bent stems
of the pansies, through the perfume of May roses,
but also over pink granules of poison
scattered by people for creatures larger than it
and considered more harmful.

The sheen of silver left on
the poison
is as perfect, as bright as that
on the roses.

We adorn each sin
in the silver of our moment,
unaware of the angel
blushing, hastening to renew our path
with pansies, with sunbeams, with roses.

Messenger

What message do you have for me
and from whom, little bird,
almost fused to the bark of the walnut tree?
Only the blue-gray sky of your collar
reveals where you cling
to the ashes of time
in which I dress myself.

A small straw-thatched
window, moon-like, is lodged
in the fog-shrouded trunk,
and on it, if I gaze through—a book
written with a prayer.
Only one.

Oh, why have you come, bird,
to perch in His light
and sweep the ashes from my path,
turning it blue once more
and full of song?

Sometimes I am the ax
in the lonely woman's hand.
Sometimes the gnarled strawberry
beside her path
                    wild and sweet.

2.

Wild Strawberries

In the Fresh Green Fjord

Outside the window, a birch.
Caught in its bare branches, an iron bed and
a portrait of the civil servant—Homer Pound, the poet's father.

Inside, the dirty elevator
with the woman fragrant as a forest,
holding a woven basket:
"Wild strawberries! Strawberries for sale!"

But I can no longer hear her cry.
Already I'm adrift on its fresh green fjord.

A cage with wild strawberries!

Winter Scene with My Parents' House

The archetypal serenity
of the dining-room table,
the quiet presence of books
and dusty phonograph records,
the careful arrangement of paintings on the wall—
I am surrounded by the day's familiar order.

In my father's faded green armchair
I recover my true self, as if midstream
in a mirror crisscrossed by rivers and a filigree
of beloved faces. The order
of my parents' house calls me
inside a circle of light, a lair
with the scent of past generations
and May lilacs that drape a blue-violet mantle
over blacker and blacker thoughts,
over the coffee grounds at the bottom of my cup,
the residue of so many lost mornings.

Here, in my parents' old house in Cotroceni,
a hidden cry bursts from the dark basement,
a moan of the soul emblazoned in spring-green
to attract that capricious harlot
answering to the name Hope.

I wish I could save its tenderness
by drawing a new-old curtain across it,
one painted with the garden of the Samurcași Monastery
where my parents lie buried. Another scene
with the beehives of my grandparents' garden in Sibiu.
Also the rush of the River Teju near El Greco's house in Toledo and
in the backyard of their house on Waring Avenue

Elizabeth picking flowers for her little brother Nicholas.
My cry floats like a zeppelin high over Bucharest—
nearer, it pirouettes like a ballerina
on the ice-cold hand of the grandmother
crouched on the sidewalk of the Boulevard of Heroes, begging.

Softly falling snow covers the Cotroceni hill
where I raced the other children
on a wooden sled my father made for me.

Then the last curtain drops
like my mother's feeble hand
against the edge of the bed.
Suddenly all becomes still
like the gradual sinking of Venice
in a silent movie.

I get up from my father's chair
and step carefully from the room
into this winter scene
made visible only now
in the steady gleam
of the candle-flame swirling
before the icon.

Convent in the Mountains

As evening falls, the nun's black habit
is darkened further by drops
of milk spilled in the morning
as she fed two orphans—a fawn
and a kid under the green darkness
of fir trees beside the shy red
of wild strawberries—pearls
and rubies of goodness
woven now into plain dark cloth
at the foot of a mountain,
sheltering somehow
the entire world.

Scene from Apold de Jos

I come from a mountain town
often washed by rain showers,
and sometimes filled with the scent
of wild strawberries or smoky wood fires.

In the morning my father
would place the bread on the table
near the clay pot filled with fresh buffalo milk
just brought from the village of Apold.
The wise eye of the sun, illuminating the window's red shutters,
quickens at the sight of this holy family
gathered around the long oak table.

On the vineyard-covered hills
surrounding my father's Apold
I used to clamber as if on a Transylvanian Acropolis
where gods, abandoning the skies,
played with us.
We'd hang cherry earrings on our ears
and pick raspberries
that glowed like bright jewels in the endless light
of childhood.

As a little boy my father used to cross these hills
every Monday morning
walking to school in Saliște,
his bag rich with the aroma of
round homemade bread, still warm.
Fresh cheese too, big as a snowball.
His books were protected in a tricolor cloth
woven by his sister Ana, her blond hair
swaying at her waist in braids.

I can almost see him laugh while he tells us
about that hot August day
he was left alone at home, absolute master
of the farmyard with the old walnut tree,
the cattle and horses in the white barn—
that egg dropped by a bird near the house,
as his mother used to say, tucking the children into bed
on old-fashioned mattresses stuffed with straw
still sweet with stars and new-mown grass
scythed by my grandfather only
under the light of a full moon.

On just such a day the gypsy Ludovica
knocked on the door to show
my father *the most beautiful needle*
in the whole world. "With this magic needle
you can sew the finest clothes
and toys that won't ever wear out.
With this needle you can mend
the great wide world when it rips
and you no longer seem to fit into it.
You can stitch your very own road
to Saliște and back.
And through its tiny window you can spy
all the oceans and seas.
I'll let you have it for almost nothing, just
whatever bread's in the house."

My father didn't think twice
and filled Ludovica's bag with bread.

In the evening when his parents came home from the fields
my father leapt up to welcome them
with the needle raised high in his small right hand

like a king displaying his scepter.
It was then his mother spoke quietly, earnestly
to him about the holiness of bread,
the work and tears
that bring bread to the family's table,
how there's no miracle to surpass
the miracle of those grains of wheat,
an offering for the living and the dead.

Now on a dreary October night
I look into my father's drawer and see, glinting near his glasses,
the watch he always wore, and near the open cigarette case —
Ludovica's needle. Like the needle of a compass
it points to the village of Apold, nestled among hills
that humbly climb toward a wooden church,
its open door and windows
fanning light out into the planet's darkness.

Growing Old

I gaze at my hands, not yet
grown ugly. My eyes
still sparkle, brightened
by joys, jeweled
by tears.

I offer my days
in unequal portions:
so much for my family,
so much for other people and the usual demands—
the kitchen, the editorial office, teaching,
my notebook of poems.
Finally, the garden
and my parents' grave.

It's spring—
I've bought flowers to plant.
More and more often I find myself bending
to the warm earth, my hands
digging in its dust.
I press soil over the tender roots
of forget-me-nots.
Then, from the well of the dead,
I draw a pail of water.
Only here, near the convent,
do the dead still have something
to call their own.

I water the newly planted flowers,
then stand and stretch my back, bend
again, try to light a memorial candle.
When the wind feeds

on the tiny flame, I shelter it
with my cupped hands,
hands so soiled with earth
I barely recognize them. At home
my own garden waits,
its flowers also in need of water and love.

I'm convinced that between two moments of life,
between two bites of food,
I'll suddenly dedicate myself to gardening.
Between a lesson on metaphysics

and a recording session for my radio program,
I let my thoughts fly into that other garden.
But my hands, so much closer
to the earth, always get there
before me, a sign of my growing old.
This is my hide-and-seek
with the earth, another kind of wisdom...

"Rejoice!" God proclaimed to the holy women
when He first revealed Himself to them
after the Resurrection.

And the garden, and the wind—even the years
I've become—cry out to me. *Rejoice! Rejoice!*

On That Island...

On that island that had no name
I stayed only one day.
But we were happy for 365 days more.

We fell into a deep sleep
watched over by three wild asses
and by the flat, farsighted eyes of a dead fish
that lured us from our dream.

Land everywhere around us.
Just land.
And us, rowing our boat, rowing
across the dry land.

Lisbon

A pale blue storm rages in my brain.
The idea of death—its sudden nubile caresses.

A young man strides
with breathtaking grace
between the bright yellow trams,
over his shoulder the black strap
of a green velvet flute case, its grip
against the stark white
of his silk shirt...

The poplars throw their last silver coins
into the mirrors of his all-knowing blood,
intensifying the lingering memory of pleasure...

Nobody is ever to come,
nobody is ever to leave this Lisbon
which chastely withdraws its light
from the poet's letters.

Truth is beyond the song of the free bird,
beyond the dreaming flesh.
To recognize it
beneath this most refined of identities,
you must tear the face from it
by its skin.

3.

Square of the Ravens

Crucified Against the May Sky

Here in your orchard, Father, such peace.
The cherry trees coyly offer
their firm flesh and sweet light.
From the stately fir you cut down,
nothing is left. Only this empty space
from which five paths
radiate. Five steady rays.

In bare feet I stand
on the cool, newly turned earth
within the heart of a star.
How close you are, Father!

The wind picks up. A little bell rings.
Like the one Mother used to ring
to call us to dinner in the evening.
You would come from the garden
carrying a basket piled high
with tomatoes and apples.
Your steady smile
was our path home.

Again I hear it, that little bell
from long ago. I hurry after it
deeper into the garden
seeking its sound, that chiming from the tops
of cherry trees
bowed to the ground
with fruit.

But here is someone half hidden
by the deep green leaves, cherries brushing

his high white hand—scarecrow
wearing your sweater,
your shirt. At the end of the stiff arm
of the sleeve, our little bell
from long ago dangles. "To keep crows away,"
Vasile tells me, grinning:
"It works."

I would need a very tall ladder to reach the crown
of the cherry tree to retrieve your clothes
and our bell.
Until I can rescue them, I sit
at your table and raise a ladder
toward you, Father—
this humble poem.

Square of the Ravens

for Tess

When people stop up a spring
and pave it over to make a parking lot,
it's no wonder
the place itself starts to hide in plain sight
and you can't find your car anymore.

Suddenly the streets around us
turn into a barren labyrinth,
trees start losing their leaves
in summer, eggs tumble from nests
and no one knows
the way back to Corbeni Square—
the Square of the Ravens
where Bucharest's carriage drivers
used to water their horses
in the flicker of gas lamps
while gossiping about their lives.
In winter they'd light a roaring fire
near the spring. Water and flames
would play in their eyes,
those images still a mirage
that soars over the city
with the eloquence of a rainbow.

Again frost bites the girls' cheeks and
carriages turn into sleighs
piled high with wolf pelts.
Maybe this is why, when the moon is full,
blue howls devour the stars above this square
at the heart of the city.

On a glorious October day near the end of the millennium
we wander these Bucharest streets
with names that are never lost:
Sword-Bearers' Street,
Circle Street,
Bread Bakers' Street,
Autumn Street—
two poets in search of a lost car
left in a small square with its murdered spring.

You bend to pick up some peacock feathers.
"The sun-bird, emblem of immortality, has alighted
on our path," I tell you, and you answer, stroking a plume,
"Its tail, curved like a fan from Toledo,
is finally giving back
all those stars once stolen from your sky."

I enter a small shop
for bread and eggs.
You are still cupping feathers
in your palm. The curious salesgirl asks you,
"What kind of bird do you have in your hand?"
"How poetry transfigures everything into life," I say to myself,
while a fan of sunlight guides our steps
toward the mystery of that place with a bird's name.

Later, during the hour of wolf-claws
and wolf-fangs, you write me from the airplane
speeding you to London. At just that moment
when the pilot lost his connection to earth,
you began to pray with the rosary beads
I'd slipped onto your wrist on St. Dimitri's day,
Patron Saint of Bucharest.
Sitting next to you was an aged explorer
returning from the jungle of Peru

who kept talking about hummingbirds.
Then you remembered
that only with prayers, only by clutching
the small stone from Medjugorje
with the face of the Virgin Mary, could you make the plane
light as a feather again, peacefully floating
on the twilight.

In Corbeni Square, the raven of the poet Tradem
and the raven of Edgar Allan Poe
perch in the window of the subterranean spring
waiting side by side to be reborn.
Their duet is lightning.
Their wings are writing this poem
for you, so far away,
wrapped in the mists of the Strait of Juan de Fuca,
boiling tea for the angels while
a girl with a needle
threaded by her mother sews her white socks
into a new pair of wings.

Road Across the Mountain

Above the road, the mountains' silence;
beneath thick ice, the river.
A cold that claws at the stars,
at their evergreen moss.
Even the wild beasts have deserted
this place, the road obliterated by snow.
Harnessed to the sleigh, three nuns—
they cannot see or hear anything.
Soundlessly they pray and pull. Pray.

In the sleigh, the old monk
can scarcely draw breath, it is so cold.
"Only a little way now to the monastery,"
he whispers. From time to time
he crosses himself. "Yes, only
a little way, bless you!"

White as far as the eye can see,
deep as mind can venture,
save for the black of their vestments.
But inside the monk's frayed bag,
held to his breast,
how the Holy Communion chalice glows!

And suddenly I remember the frail grandmother
on the outskirts of town,
hardly able to drag her load of firewood home
through snow. Stooped and helpless,
she stops in the middle of the road,
lifts her eyes and shouts,
*"God, Your sky is swirling with angels.
Send me one!"*

As if at a sign, three men appear
to help her.

In the icy dead of night
the monastery gleams against the mountains.

To Father Cleopa

What is the connection
between the anchorite's moss-covered door
and this comfortable day in my room
with a color TV and soft, thick carpets?
What binds or lets fray
this communion?

The holy man's words, though unuttered,
can still be heard. They permeate
the forest, sweetening the air
with snows yet to fall.
"May Heaven engulf you"—whispered
in your ear. And the hardwood echo
of these words recalls
the syncopation of a monastery *toaca*
from long ago: *Patience,*
be patient, oh patient, patience…

A thread of smoke rises
from the mound of dead leaves in the forest
like an inward smile released
by the one who climbs the mountain
toward the Cross and bears His thought
back down to us.

An angel passes, cradling in its wingless arms
the anchorite's moss-covered door.

Pilgrimage to Outeiro

A flock of sheep drifts lazily down the hill toward the sea.
A boy with an angel on his shoulder
plays the shepherd's pipe—exactly the landscape
to heal even the blackest soul.

On the way to Outeiro
a window secretly accompanies me.
In it, a serene haiku
sketched by a blackbird—its calligraphy
of wings, its graphite song.
My friends point out the church on the horizon,
our destination.
We are following the old road of the pilgrims.

Within the living soul of the church
the body of the martyr, Saint Quintino, reposes
alive as ever. We arrive
and the desert of the hot afternoon
almost engulfs us.

An old woman in a white scarf emerges
from a car with no wheels,
in her hand a huge brass key.
Crossing herself, she opens the church doors,
then sits quietly in the corner
near the still smoking candles
as I say my prayer.

When I turn to go outside to the darkness,
she draws me down an aisle,
gripping my hand.
I feel the calluses of her rough palm

but also beneficial warmth.
In silence she points ahead:
and oh, the azure pelerine of the Virgin Mary
which adorns her statue for the great procession,
the dazzling white robes of the priests,
the silver chalice, and—finally, held out to us
for our redemption
just this side of the sacred—
                    the child-sized communion spoon.

Wingless Victory

"I am no longer a bird in your palm."
—*Shara McCallum*

Near the dead whom we loved,
writing paper turns damp by the sea
like our eyes and clothes.
Below, smoke threaded with spirits
of the departed, candles flicker
along the shore—tiny mirrors
for the light of stars.

Under the little girl's foot, a pyramid.
Under the other, a butterfly.
She bursts into laughter.
The divine laughter of statues.

The graying of the cosmos starts at my left temple.
A blade of grass tattoos my right,
here at the end of the second millennium after Christ.

From the salt of tears spring the wings
of the goddess "Victory."
People have torn the possibility of flight
from her, hoping to keep her with them
always. But wings without victory
are no better than victory without wings—
as in my wingless liberty
in an almost lost marriage
in an almost Mediterranean city.

Scene with Wash on a Clothesline

All my neighbors have hung their wash out to dry,
a sign spring is at hand.

Suddenly I see the bent man
who toiled forty years
in the lead mines of Siberian prison camps.
When he was freed
and they offered him a patch of land
and a small cottage there,
he refused.

Instead he returned to Romania,
to the Galați of his youth,
where he found none of his family alive.

Now he lives on a pension and sleeps in a hotel in Sighet
where he became museum guide at the biggest
former political prison in Europe.
When asked his deepest wish
since gaining freedom, he replied:

> "To be able to hang my clean wash out to dry
> on a clothesline in spring. To bury my face,
> my lips, my closed eyes in fresh linen,
>   and to forget."

An Existential Alphabet

As if I were passing
through the desert of a closed door
to pick armfuls of white poppies
along the shoulder of a parched road
and howling, not at the moon,
but at my helplessness
before my mother's suffering.

As if beyond the door
stood a pyramid of ice, and
hidden inside it, an egg of wax,
and trembling at the center of its transparent yolk,
on a single spear of grass,
a tear—more diaphanous than light
and pregnant with the letter *A*.

Seeds of Sun Rays

At dusk, near the carved wooden gate
of a holy monastery, a toothless peasant woman
smiles mysteriously and gives me seeds
neatly wrapped in newspaper.
"Seeds of sun rays," she whispers,
then hurries to catch the last bus
back to her high mountain village.

I am rooted to the spot,
the bright seeds cupped in my grasp
as if in a dream, not daring to move
for fear I might wake to darkness,
my hands empty.

Illumination

I fall,
I get up,
I fall again,
and I try to cling to the light
with fingers of wax.

I would trade my worldly sadness
for a small window
through which the world
could be seen far off
as prayer. Only You, God, would be shining
through that window ...

In what dark colors
I bathed my younger years!

With an angel holding my hand, I learned
to walk again.
With my eyes fixed on the sky,
I transformed my sins into the white silk
of a prayer shawl. Exchanged the red
of pain for the gold of tears.

To Mother Alexandra

founder of the Orthodox Monastery of the Holy
Transfiguration, Ellwood City, Pennsylvania
—for her soul

Perhaps imitating earth itself,
mysterious in what it hides,
the golden globe reflects
green fir branches. But our smiles,
those garlands of gladness
at the birth of our Lord Jesus Christ,
are multiplied even more brightly.

In the same way, a holy monastery
now gleams, turning before my soul
like that globe on the Christmas tree
of my girlhood. Everything is contained
in its tender sphere: cells
for the nuns, the tiny church
built of wood and holiness, deepened
by the joy of His omnipresence.

The nun Haritina is handing me
a gift: a small icon of the Virgin Mary
framed for me with her own hands.
Behind glass she has added a clover leaf
and a dried pansy with its three petals
still deep red, picked last summer
from the garden sheltering
this fragment of sky,
the Monastery of the Holy Transfiguration.

Mother Theodora, from far away
near the Danube, raised within the light

of the Romanian language and the heart
of the Virgin Mary, welcomes me
with a shy smile, her black habit spattered
with red and blue pigment: in the mystery of prayers
offered in her cell, she has been painting
the Last Supper. She leads me into the tiny wooden church—
a ship crossing the sea of mountains in Pennsylvania.
I kneel, cloistered in the gold of the holy liturgy
with humility and happiness
near these nuns.
Although they have nothing that is their own,
they look as though they have everything.

As I leave, in the small orchard near the gate
another nun is pruning apple trees:
"Don't feel sorry for these trees. Whatever I cut
will make space for a new bud, then

a new flower, and a year later, a new apple."
In a patch of snow, twigs have piled up
at her feet. Small heaps of golden apples…
Suddenly she includes me in her wise smile
and whispers, as if to herself,
her voice jeweled in the ice of a late spring storm and,
like a bud bursting open: *You
are here to remember—
and I, to learn.*

written January 27, 1998, at the Monastery

4.

New Moon With Poets

Summer Story in Altoona Winter

After five years, at a time when
I no longer knew which hand
was my right, which
my left, and I was slowly drowning—
my destiny brought me back to America,
to the town hidden under the eyelid of a mountain.
Here my friend from the other side of the Danube
teaches cultural geography,
a course about why a young farmer suffers
when displaced to a city,
or how the lack of water can launch
wars more vast than the Trojan War.
No wonder the loaves of fresh bread she bakes
give off an aroma
of too much solitude.

In the center of the Altoona Campus—
a small lake policed by a flock
of Canada geese and by the carols
which take flight from a bell tower
where the ancient astronomer
still studies the blessed star
the Magi followed.

It's evening, it's December.
A horse-drawn carriage rattles down the hill.
Happily we climb on
and, with tears mixed with snowflakes,
I can hardly whisper:
"I think I'm going to be born once again,
this time in the middle of a fairy tale."

And I tell Marieta the story
of the July evening in Sibiu
when Father took Mother to the maternity hospital
in a carriage because I was impatient
to see the big world, to travel along
its slippery spine toward more
and more mysterious lands.

I had to wait forty-eight years
and cross an ocean
to ride once again
in a carriage
pulled by a pair of draft horses.
And to breathe steam rising from hot bread
and witness the steam glistening as frost on horses' manes.

Such a long way
to see my mother once more,
red-cheeked, happy, feeding me at her breast
in the light of wildflowers
picked by my father the evening before—
once upon a time in July,
in Europe,
in Sibiu…

December Journey from Pennsylvania to Florida

to my son Mihnea

We're starting on our way to Florida, my feet cold
despite new boots. The car keeps skidding
as we creep into the gray of the December morning, but even so,
we arrive at the station early. Ice glitters threateningly
on the empty platform and the doors
of the small red-brick building are locked,
a dream without a key in my special year in Pennsylvania, 1997.

"They don't open till half an hour before the train,
the only one still connecting the West Coast with the East,"
a man explains, wrapped warmly in clouds of smoke.
As for us, East Europeans hunkered against the cold and used
to waiting, we simply stand
in the thickly falling snow. But you,
my sixteen-year-old son, keep asking impatiently,
"When does the station open?"
I blow my warm breath over your hands, red with cold,
try to joke, "There's no longer a train, only a moon rocket!"

Finally, a girl with boots red as poison mushrooms after a warm rain
opens the little station. She makes coffee and tea, $1.50 a cup,
and ham sandwiches. You want tea and a dusty postcard of Miami.
The young woman near us, a baby in her arms,
tells us she's going to her sister's; she's in the middle of a divorce.
Another, her hair tawny as a lioness, shows us scars on her face.
"They're all I've got after twenty years of marriage in Wisconsin.
I'm heading south to pick oranges. At least I can get rid
of this hat, these boots, and my crazy Mark."

The only one silent is a an older man who watches
the rest of us, a Vietnam vet whom nothing
surprises. Suddenly a shrill train whistle
scatters us. Everybody quickly tosses plastic cups
and sandwich scraps, hurries to the platform. The girl
with red boots locks up again.
And the conscientious snow slowly sifts over
our footsteps, our waiting, our words and stories.

In the train's warmth, you immediately slump
into a dream of the great train stations of the world
while I recall the little railroad stop in an Apold winter,
hidden among hills, its lights
aglow all night, the station agent stoking wood into the stove
and telling us, as if we were his own children,
"Be good, my dears. God will take care of you."

Through the window I watch America rushing alongside us.
Then I take out my little book from home. It opens at random:
"And so, in that monastery, some of the young monks
used to eat only the food left on their plates by the aged fathers.
In this way, they became blessed."

A Visit to Peleş Castle, Seen from Pennsylvania

for Helen Dunmore and Mircea Ivănescu

A barbaric spring.
Snow knee deep.
Knees which should have
undertaken a pilgrimage to Fatima.
A group of writers in Romania,
purveyors of illusion, opening the path
to Peleş Castle in the town of Sinaia.
Words mantled in silence,
violet silk shawls conjured
by the young poet in open sandals
as she whispers, "Oh, this snow makes me shiver!"

"Snow of the lambs!"—a voice
muffled by snow.

We are hiking in the mountains side by side,
the poet from Sibiu in our tracks, Mircea
with his retinue of know-it-all cats,
his pockets filled with the seeds of sun rays.
Silver-haired and myopic, the essence
of absence, he caresses the nervous sea
in some indolent, loose-limbed poem.

Here in Pennsylvania,
the sun sinks low
over the dying notes of a Chopin nocturne.
In my mind I strike the spark of a star
on the boundary between pond and garden,

near the yellow water lily,
the last melted candles sputtering, then
five lazy red carp
and the black cape
thrown over a startled rabbit
who turned up out of nowhere
in the middle of this poem
peopled with poets from far away
in Sinaia and Sibiu.

In the royal palace of Peleş—silk carpets
on which our shadows lose their way...
such stories embedded in the weft
knotted by slaves.
If they finished in time
they were freed.
Work too slowly—
their eyes were plucked out.

Caged in the room painted by Klimt,
a wardrobe with a thousand drawers—
on each the painting of a bird.
I can still hear a wing beat,
a flutter of song
intimating flight to warmer lands.

But here in my apartment, near Mount Nittany,
the evening advances steadily,
silently, like the tongue of an iceberg.

A Parrot, Dreaming

A bright yellow parrot screams
in a black cage.
With each scream, he strikes the bars.
Flies. And keeps flying,
strumming until the bars run red,
staining the sunset. The exhausted bird
can hardly breathe, dreaming
of freedom, an exercise of flight
glimpsed between the bars.
Even the grass shrieks
as his feathers, suddenly gray,
fall to earth.

In the same way,
any featherless heart
heaped under snow
may, in the brief freedom
of a prayer, be resurrected
breath by breath.

Small Fires in the Dusk

Is it the whisper of wild strawberry leaves
that baptizes the earth with sweet-scented light?
I bow over the moon's contour, white on my page,
this eggless nest woven of words.

The hollow paw-print of a fox in the soft green moss—
a transitory, wild impression,
like their living absence, the departed
brushing my ankle.

Color Study

for Lena Pasternak

Green hill, yellow hill.
And here, close by the road, a red tile roof,
its insignificant pyramid
stretching my sight to the horizon.

A train whistle—
the shrillest of dividing lines,
its slice of blue,
separates these June landscapes
which don't want, don't ask
to be described, but quietly
let themselves be ignored.

The solitude of the blackbird,
of the wave, of silent dew
bathing a flower that still refuses to open.
These are real and describable—yes,
only as far away as despair,
as joy.

Easter-Lily Bulbs

"What lovely Easter lilies on your shoulder!"
The old woman smiles
and, uncomprehendingly,
I smile back. Suddenly I remember
my coat—its print of tiny, perfect lilies.
During an autumn with few stars
and fewer dying flowers
I had bought it in the discount store
at the foot of Mount Nittany, named
by the Indians. Lilies worn
like a suit of armor
or a dream-catcher in the form of
matching earrings, a dangling
medallion, or a loosened hairpin.

In a Bucharest ravished
by an autumn of starless nights,
I've returned home to start
my journey all over again
between yesterday and tomorrow
on my path toward God.

Today my neighbors phoned to offer
Easter lilies for my garden.
On a morning shrouded by fog, I open
the ground to plant the bulbs
near a lonely brick wall
covered by ivy.

I don't know if these lilies
will push through earth to bloom next spring.
But already the firm white flesh of their light
enfolds my blackest hour.

Telescope Trained on Monticello and Apold

The fallen egg of a bird, broken
into the dark forest among snowdrops,
breathing shyly under barren April rain.

Slowly the sky flows out of the mouth of America.
Daffodils light up this patch of land
holding Jefferson and his descendants.
"Father of a Nation": smudged alphabet
buried in the Valentine-heart
of a little girl.

The white of the guide's blouse reflects
the sumptuous mansion.
In the valley below, cherry trees blossom
among faint stirrings of spring.
(The hiss of snails, feathers
floating from nests, the scratching of claws
on a sapling's smooth bark.)

The death of two fathers suffuses this spring
with the mystery of beginnings: both
gardeners; one an engineer
from the Balkans, the other
president of a nation; both heads
of a family. They are an invisible thread
tying Romania to Virginia, Apold to Monticello:
the human laws of history, challenged by souls
bridging continents swollen and curved
like two tears—an infant's, a mother's—
united by an alchemy that transforms

any metal into gold, any language
into light.

I have passed the skyscrapers of America,
the perfectly lit McDonald's.
I have wandered through the glass canyons of Manhattan
and crossed the panoramic green of Pennsylvania.

Heaven and earth shall pass away, but my words
shall not pass away.
Throughout the whole of our great journey,
these words reverberate.

The two earthly gardeners have always kept
a telescope trained on the heavens
in order to log into a journal
the everyday lives of plants
from which derive both goodness and humility,
but also to record the egg, dashed
among snowdrops. The painful mystery
of simply being a father.

For Ann, on Her Birthday

In the depths of winter
my pencil is sweet with hyacinths.
The lion has lain down in the desert
to sleep at the Saint's feet.
Only a shy pink light separates our worlds,
seasons, words.

On her birthday Ann
hiked up the mountain
just to follow the stream
to its waterfall.

She glories in heights.
She liked most
helping to raise the cupola
above the church in Williamsport.

In her white nurse's coat
she breezes through the hospital
like a cloud of hyacinths,
melting the ice around the sickbeds,
bringing peace
into frightened eyes,
into lost bodies.

She always keeps
the names of stars, the lit candles
reflecting her mother's prayers
or early morning footsteps in the kitchen,
her father's smile, as warming to her as fresh bread,
while he paints the red Easter eggs.

In the depths of winter
my pencil is sweet with hyacinths
because it has written these lines
for Matthew
for Evelyn
for Ann.

October 29, 2003,
Lewisburg, PA

New Moon with Poets

I climb the hill on Pugh, descend
on Garner or Allen, streets
with strange foreign names,
with secrets hidden in each doll's house.
But where is the old Ibsen to describe them?
Where, the young Dostoevsky to disclose them?
Or a Faulkner to close them into history again?

I live temporarily in this American town
as if in a small and captivating theater,
with fairy-tale decor and actors, both good and bad.
My room is always in half-darkness,
I'm the anonymous spectator in a velvet armchair
under the bell jar of a tiny town, dreaming of life
far from any happy valley.

Europe is somewhere in the wings,
folded in dusty tourist brochures.
It's the silver tinsel of Mozart and Enescu,
my Sibiu a small dot on the map
in the arms of the Carpathian mountains.

The moon's thin sickle is about to slice
the threads from which a star hangs,
a trapeze on which poets without watches
or borders perform
with no safety net, with neither cheers
nor encouragement. Every night
they swing high above the abyss
of this world, beautiful and free, soaring
over our bodies immersed in sleep.

New moon, new moon,
climb with me on Allen,
descend with me on Pugh or Garner,
and turn your sickle
into a cradle.

Only if rocked will the stars
let down their silver ladders
on which, from time to time,
the dreamers descend to earth
from their royal sadness.

5.

I Refuse to Write About My Heart

I Refuse to Write About My Heart

I can describe anything easily:
this American room so unlike my home,
its panes of glass that don't open outward,
won't draw inward—
Well, lucky me: I have a compass in my blood.
I'll never suffer claustrophobia.

I can describe this existentialist armchair
or the glazed eye of the TV.
We coexist in reciprocal disdain.
I can describe immaculate houses,
the spoiled puppets who pass in and out
after jogging, after the work day, after sex—
perfectly coiffed, perfectly manicured,
perfectly alone.

I can even describe their allergies, their reliance
on the Internet with its grand deception:
one can go anywhere one chooses,
enter any dwelling, any room without a trace,
get into contact with Proust, Ibsen, Madonna,
or with the rich, emerald green moss eclipsing
the house of the most recent Nobel Prize winner.

I can describe my awkward battle against my camera:
I'm atechnical, always told I have two left hands.
I wanted to preserve what I could of my week in Princeton
between Picasso's prismatic eye and
Henry Moore's enveloping arms—I mean
their sculptures, of course—
and in twenty-four color photographs,
thousands of black and white words,

my image of the rain on your cheek,
of my life inside this blood-worn clock
that doesn't measure hours, seconds or millennia.
Only what will never count—this distance
between us.

San Francisco

Dawn, and the morning star sips at the grass.
This moment of serenity at the center of my soul
in the city of the saint of Assisi
beside the Pacific Ocean
becomes a wreath of jasmine.

Only the ocean licks the silence
of salt,
of alabaster,
of green.

Only in the angel
who keeps watch over you
would the night bury
its jewels.

I climb the steep hills
clutching the spiral of the here and now.
Then the streets lead me down to the bay
and a rope of white silk stretches
between this city and me, between
sequoia and cedar. My past
walks across with care,
invisible but palpable

like great pain
after great love.

City Lights

To climb a staircase
along which the word POETRY ascends
on risers. To wear brochures
from the Church of St. Francis of Assisi
in the pocket over your heart
next to a cable-car ticket
for streets that also climb
                              high, then higher.

Like a stage set—
the sea, a painted backdrop at the far end
                              of the street and,
mirrored from the near end
of your famished memory—again the sea.

To reach the Poetry Room, its walls
cracked by so many earthquakes within,
discovering there, through the bars of the fire escape,
laundry hung to dry outside its window: shirts, diapers, bras
and a plush, pale yellow rabbit dangling by its ears—
these are the only birds that still alight
in this far corner of the world.

A rope of clothes lifted, carried, then released by wind—
a train made up of small ordinary lives
hurtling past without a glance
toward the Poetry Room
with its smoky wooden shelves,
and Walt Whitman, like the patron saint
of a wayside shrine, smiling mysteriously
from the sepia photograph.

Or Allen Ginsberg,
his HOWL tucked neatly beneath his arm
but sprouting huge wings that fan
his black-rimmed eyeglasses, and
under pages and pages of poetry, his body
tattooed with an American flag.

The aroma of books mingles
with the greasy thumbprint-smell
of french fries, just as when gamblers
shuffle a deck of cards
to mix the black-and-blood of their lives.

No, I am not here to cry out or weep,
but to listen to the pain of others,
finding words that enter the bloodstream.
Not to console myself
but, if I can, like the voices here in this room,
to console others.

San Francisco—crazy city. Pale
like Baudelaire in the morning, tender
as Tsvetaeva's smile
before she interrupts her poem at the cry
of her baby who dreams of her breasts, their twin
burdens of milk. Answers of the moment
for doubts to come.

City raging high over the ocean.
City tamed once in a while
by the voice of the poet.

City Lights Bookstore,
March 20, 1998

The Antique Shop

Diaphanous in dandelion light,
the antique shop on the hill
shimmers with the bric-a-brac of everyday life
glinting from dining room tables, armchairs,
chests of drawers, souvenir coffee mugs,
translucent glass beads.

In one corner I discover a carriage
heaped with dolls, their eternal blue eyes,
the apricot blush of their cheeks.
They are the same age as my mother
when she so badly wanted the doll she never got.

As a child, depriving herself of the family's walk
each weekend to the "Roman Emperor" patisserie,
she finally made herself
a rag doll with button eyes sacrificed
from her Sunday dress.

I leave the antique shop
pushing the carriage—
inside, the most beautiful doll.

I long for my mother so much
I've gone into every antique shop
from New York to Sibiu.
I can't stop buying dolls, more dolls!
Someday I'll find just the right one
with bone-button eyes.

And I try on dress after dress
until I find the yellow one with wild daisies
my mother used to wear when I was a girl,
and the pink one with matching scarf Mother wore
that day I gave birth to my son.

Seeds Along a Forgotten Road

When I was a little girl, I liked so much
the story of the two children sent into the forest
by the poor wood-cutter and his wife
so they would become lost.
But the children secretly dropped pebbles, crumbs of bread
and seeds to mark their path home.

Today, on the way to the Altoona campus,
Marieta stops here and there to show me places
that mark her daily commute: a country store
full of apples, a bakery
with steaming pretzels, the small branch
post office hidden behind brooms
and tools in a hardware store.
"I send letters from here to my son in Rila"—
a kind of sacred topos
only mothers know by heart.

Every day Marieta scatters seeds
along this forgotten road
in Pennsylvania. Maybe that's why her son
on the road to Rila always senses,
buried under the deep drifts
of Bulgarian snow, the muffled red
of live poppies by which
he finds his way home.

Autumn Poem

In September it's humiliating
to chase away memory. Don't hide
your face from me—more leaves
still must fall!

The madwoman gathers chestnuts from the hill
and sets her shadow on fire,
then her loose gray hair…

Once you asked me if I had ever caressed a statue.
I laughed, and pried the small silver fish
from your hook.

How it twitched
on the palm of my hand
with the memory of oceans.

Dorothy Two Years Later

I found her in a nursing home in Pennsylvania.
Excited she has someone to talk to, she asks,
"Look at the cage and tell me—
do the birds really have chicks
as the nurses keep saying?
Your eyes are good, not like ours.
Maybe it's another of their lies."

She's Valentine's Day Queen.
In her wheelchair, a silver-foil crown on her head,
she wants to know if I'm still living in America or did I
go home. Maybe I still remember
that gray Saturday in December
when she pulled the fire alarm, so lonely
she wanted someone to dance with . . .

When I leave, Dorothy stares at the floor.
"Come see me again. Come read me poetry.
And please tell everybody
you're my daughter from across the ocean.
Tell the others, too, that the birds
really have babies, even in our nursing home,
even here in captivity."

The Poet's Table

Beneath the crystal table—
a sea, a green sky,
a grove of orange trees.

And nested in each tree,
playing with a dazzling mirror—
an ecstatic blind angel.

6.

Longing for the Sea

Eating Grapes in February

I am reminded of the vineyard in Apold,
my father and his brother setting out
for the hillside early in the morning,
plodding ahead on the wagon
where their sister Ana had put
the steaming *mămăligă* for them
along with the disembodied smile
of white cheese like a crescent moon
grinning at the last star in the sky.

Here in Kentucky
the hills are bald elephants
carrying people, houses, foxes,
tobacco—words like stones
tied around the necks of the drowned.

What luck to have a yellow bird
sitting on her nest, patient, aristocratic, wise—
like Sarah playing the piano
while telling me about her mother.
Outside the grass freezes into a skating rink
on which a last word
left behind by carefree summer
swirls round and round in a waltz.

I open Sarah's book of poems and all at once
as in a fairy tale
a low honeyed fire
illuminates each poem,
glows even on her hands
that washed her dying mother's white hair
and also the blond braids of her daughter

to whom she gave birth
in the shade of a laurel tree
between earth and an ocean.

I take another grape, another.
I eat my way back to the vineyard.
My father puts into my palm the blue-violet cascade
fresh from the vine.

Spring in St. Matthew District

A jewelry box lined with silk:
the layer-cake sky—white, blue, gray.
Trees, where angels cavort in spring, become
dull lead soldiers. Sparks
from their celestial tournaments hiss out, then
plunge here and there onto lawns: crocuses
singeing our hearts. And those snowdrops
that renew compassion with a tear—
in their crystal sphere, I am allowed, Mother,
to meet again your sweet gaze.

Poem with a White Feather and Two Streets

What remains of Saint Stephen Street
in Bucharest?
The memory of my mother slicing
a watermelon into equal new moons.
My father shaving the long block of ice,
patiently inching it
into our small icebox.
And the white lilac outside our window—
does it still bless each morning in our district
so crowded with churches and statues?

What still remains of Steven Street
from my spring in Louisville?
The small houses—blue, pink, yellow—
fragrant with myrtle and jasmine.

A white feather floats back
and forth between these two streets—
saving everything
that can be
saved.

Our words after heavy rainfall,
mysteriously turning green.

Louisville, 4 May 2000

The Perfect Street

Could it be the Orient Express, every compartment lit,
emerald green champagne bottles on the tables,
women wearing exotic perfumes
posed at each window?

The Champs Elysée, Broadway, Cherokee Road,
Calea Victoriei—streets that pale
in the face of the tenderness
of small houses in which we accomplish
what the world puts off. Their cozy rooms
are chocolate truffles melting on the sky
of your mouth in an evening
of dry lighting.

The Via Appia, Puerta del Sol, Evia—
all bow before your armada,
acacias armed with white blossoms.

You are the ideal street.
You have only fourteen houses
and the brand of your perfume
is "Spring-in-the-Woods."
You spoil us with a house
for each day of the week:

The Monday house

where we meet to read poems
about postponed lives, borrowed
lives, invented lives.

The Tuesday house
where we take shelter from rain
in the light of a bird
rescued because this is the street
of rescue. There we forget
to grow old.

The Wednesday house
when my body
is as mysterious and invisible
as the moon before it rises from sea.

The Thursday house
where I wrap my hands
gently around your heart.
Like a sister, a mother,
a daughter, I whisper to you,
"Don't be afraid,

don't ever be afraid,
even if you are pierced by a splinter
from the mirror, even if
you go blind, staring at
your life in the desert."

The Friday house
where you always paint the same painting:
*The birds of paradise sing
but don't let us into heaven.*
In ornate calligraphy I draw their echo
on each of my hands,

on each of your words.

The Saturday house
encloses your town and mine,
your river and my river,
your cat and my cat
and Pegasus, the horse of fortune
bearing us beyond our lives.

The Sunday house
is full of icons.
Nothing belongs to us here anymore
yet everything is somehow still ours.

As to the other seven houses,
they hold the lives of all the world's poets
and all the years when I'm no longer with you.
You'll get dizzy trying to live in them
because every evening
I must return for exactly an hour
to dance with you.
                          Then,
to become as light and buoyant as possible,
we'll throw away the stars in our pockets.
The gardens of the perfect street
will become an immense inverted sky,
a sky that knows not to be jealous
of our divine wound.

The perfect street?
Just a keepsake
from a traveler like me,
a trinket I place next to your coffee cup
every morning
instead of your first cigarette.

Room 411

She loves the plant with fleshy leaves,
and those thick sandwiches.
"Oh, that other plant's too delicate," she complains
between bites. "It's called Wandering Jew
and, to me, it doesn't say a thing. It needs
so much care. I have to remove
sickly leaves all the time."

I tell myself inaudibly
that they look like the skinny arms of orphans
on the streets of Bucharest
when they reach out and cry "Mama"
to any passerby, woman or man.

Immediately I take the plant
to my borrowed desk,
with its locked drawers
and its view of Mount Nittany.
If I don't take it, who will?
If one angel hadn't adopted me
a long time ago, on a perfect July day,
who else?

Longing for the Sea

She has never left her mountains.
Everything she sees in the morning
repeats itself by evening:

the hot udder swollen with milk, scent of hay
and bluebells, the warm yellow *mămăligă*
swimming in its eye of milk,
the flock of sheep climbing, then drifting
in a cloud down the mountainside,
and the statue-like shepherd resting his chin on his staff
like the Neolithic thinker of Hamangia.
From time to time he barters his soul
for a melody on the panpipes
or a bottle of plum or apricot brandy.

She has never left her mountains.
Under her pillow her grandsons found her Bible
on which she made a cross every night
before she went to sleep. From it, hundreds of yellowed scraps
of paper drift like snow onto the floor,
those wooden planks she scrubbed with water
carried in a heavy bucket from the river
and sweetened with basil flowers.
On each ragged piece of paper she has drawn
one message:
a ship . . .

7.

Word Shadow

Romanian Ars Poetica

You cannot dream or write poetry
unless you've waited a lifetime
like Ovid for the same ship,
and unless you can describe the reoccurring red bird,
or maybe it's blue—though in your country's sky
the birds are only gray and black.

The Sand of Olimp

I am translating the poems of George Szirtes
on a skittish afternoon in early May.
Near my feet, a kitten, its eyes just opened,
wobbles its first steps.
The shadow of the flowering raspberry canes
creeps slowly along my leg
while somebody strides triumphantly
across my shadow,
somebody from the past.

On the white table in the garden, my eyeglasses,
a dictionary, Cavafy, *The Bestiary* of Helen Dunmore,
The Lives and Works of the Great Saints.

I open the big, brightly colored umbrella.
At this moment I translate the last lines,
about the accordion player and the blind intellectual,
with the closing phrase, "Be wise, be good."
Evening falls. I shut the umbrella.

Suddenly, everything is salted with fine sand,
touched by the beach and by the sea, wintered together
there in the folds of my umbrella.
Now they sift onto this May freshness,
over the finale of my day—ethereal, beatific,
as if an angel unfurled its wings.

The Night Comes Riding

on a wolf's grizzled back.
Happy is the woman who saves Enkidu
from the realm of the beasts.
But happier are you when you snatch me
from words and take my heart for meat
inside four walls.

Prayer for Nettles

Stars still speckle the sky
as I wake, splash my face with cold water
from the well beside the lilac bush
and set out to gather young nettles.

I can hear the cuckoo's song.
Only now, when the beech tree's earliest buds
burst open, is its tongue
released into song.

I bend to the nettles
and in my mind ask forgiveness
before picking their soft new leaves.

To whom should I bow down
when I begin each new poem,
asking forgiveness for each word
I pluck from above? They say
the moment the cuckoo leaves off singing,
it changes into a hawk.

Sfumato

Although he left a long time ago
to live alone in the forest,
the flame of the icon lamp in his cell
has never gone out.

February with the Poet

The dull gray light of ragged February
settles into a beggar's frayed, patched skirt.
Her outstretched palm—not a single coin.
Not even a tear.

Out of nowhere a rail-thin man appears,
his black overcoat unbuttoned.
This is the poet.
But nobody on this foggy street in the Balkans
knows who he is
until flocks of cardinals
flutter from his pockets in every direction,
flames licking the frozen heart
of each passerby.

A policeman blows his whistle
and screams: "Hey, you! Where
in this dreary city
did you find
such blood-red birds?"

Photographs of Gabriela Mistral

When you were young and unknown
he used to pose you
framed by oleander in the palm-reader's garden
or at the window scattering breadcrumbs
for pigeons. So many years
have passed and nobody
takes your photograph anymore.

Later, you were awarded the Nobel Prize,
and your country stamped your image
onto a small one-peso coin.

Today, forty-five years after your death,
the national bank is issuing a new
5000-peso bill—on it
your likeness at twenty
when you poured your heart out
into long love letters,
not a coin in your pocket.
As for your lover, next to you
in the black-and-white photo
taken at the Santiago railroad station—
they cut him out.

Love Song

Mist is my squire
this late September afternoon.
Balancing a crystal tray, you offer me
an orchard of tangerines.
I call you *un chevalier de la bonne espérance.*
Somebody approaches with two goblets of ruby-red wine.
Could it be Ovid?
Orpheus?

Diskettes clatter from your pockets:
books, fjords, houses, worn-out lives.
You go on describing to me
the tradition of making a toast in your country.

"First, two people gaze into each other's eyes—
ages pass between their irises,
love stories such as never before
and never again on earth.
After this they clink glasses,
drink, then disappear
into each other's eyes again."

Meanwhile, through the curtained window,
I watch the dusty road,
an emptiness longing for
your slender body. You, in turn,
long for my youthful face
in the dying light, the flowing iris
of the Danube.

Destined for the Word

At night, near the edge of the sea
the shadow of a solitary woman on the sand
is denser than the shadow
even water could make of her.

Above here, legions of shadows promenade
along the dike: the shadow
of a white sphere,
the shadow of the dream.

Deep beneath the waves, the poet writes
the same word again and again.
This is why the whitecaps
foaming onto the shore
become free letters, horses
without reins that strike
against our gate with hooves
of gold, of copper, of crystal,
of tattered newspaper,
of sunlight.

Daughter of the word,
I bite into word-shadow,
nourish myself with the light around it…

8.

A Path to the Sea

A Path to the Sea, or the Letter A

In the morning all things in their place:
first the heart, next the coffee
steaming in its white cup, the roses
baptized with dew from the May sky—
and now the shadow of a fleeting thought
which, for such a long time,
has been circling me.

Without a whisper it alights
on my welcoming page, like sand
to a shore scrubbed by the sea—one moment
enriched, the next
impoverished.

Freed of my life,
the poem takes my place
in the garden
near a small secret door
opening onto the sea.

All things in their place. Yet nothing
what it was.

Secret Journey

Poets always meet

You live in a white apartment,
its light opaque like milk,
your impeccable white suits,
raincoats like bright sea spume,
all neatly hung in big white wardrobes
with crystal doors.

Between us lie shadows, chalk-white—
our souls' pale ghosts. Poor slaves of oblivion.
On the long white table, a simple bouquet—
lilies-of-the-valley and two lit candlesticks
like twin sun rays.

The tapestry in your room twitters with woven birds.
The books you wrote—small, silent pyramids—
house the soul of your youth.
Unchanged. Good. Tender. At peace.

In the window a birch,
the flat lazy water of the bay,
and a souvenir from the Cişmigiu Park
of my Bucharest girlhood
when its small lake used to freeze
and, so happy to see snow,
I'd go skating with my father—
a white angel held my hand
while I spun pirouettes. My father
waited for me on the shore
holding a thermos of hot tea.

You wait for me in the doorway
of your sitting room. I arrive,
or don't arrive.
And with the most natural gesture in the world,
I embrace you. Then you slowly
take off my gloves, brush the crystalline snowflakes
from my hair and blow over me
words in an unknown language.
You take my hand in yours
and seat me in a white armchair
near the stove covered with glazed white ceramic tiles.

You start telling me about your life,
the thousand years without me,
the gold of the Goths,
the man in that painting—
a warrior, your grandfather
who built his own boats—
and his wife, your grandmother,
who smelled of milk, of babies, of lavender,
her lips stained pink by the strawberries
that perfumed the short summers.

I am listening to their story
when suddenly you stand
and play a recording of Dvořák's "Cypresses."
Then you fall silent
and stare a long time out the window:
somebody's waving at you from another world,
trying to tell you something.
You sit down sadly, complain to me
how much your knees hurt.
And I realize I'm out of place
in your new white apartment with a view of the bay.

But before going I tell you a story:
of the woman in my mountains
who, one hard winter,
sold her amber earrings
for a cartful of wood
or of my grandfather
who, during World War II,
sold his garden in Sibiu
for a bag of potatoes
or of my grandfather in Apold
who used to write home from the front
on birch bark.

Hey hey hey! my Balkans,
the aroma of smoke and basil,
of cabbage and the meat in *sarmale*,
of mutton pastrami
and brash new wine.

Hey hey hey! the first crocus of spring
eaten as communion
by the shepherds on the mountain peaks.

Hey hey hey! a violin made from an orange crate
by Brâncuși at eighteen.

Hey hey hey! Alexander the Great
who at eighteen commanded
the Macedonian cavalry.

Hey hey hey! the Danube's waves,
the joy of knowing that someone you can't forget
always waits for you.

Requiem for a Wasp

Thistles stick to my blue skirt,
small suns, prickly fallen stars
from the seashore that cling
like orphans braced against
oncoming winter.

Suddenly as I write
I feel the throb
in my thumb from the wasp
that died two weeks ago
aboard that ship on the Danube
when the surging of the great river
washed my past, present and future away,
and also my mother's lap
where I used to hide
both my joy and my solitude.

Today I walked through my city,
on streets with strange names:
The Garden with Horses,
The Well with Poplars, The Haymarket—
not knowing I moved
with so much light on my skirt,
and in my finger
so much forgetting…

A Walk on the Shore

You stand sentry, a Roman soldier
weary of war, your melancholy face
singed by a foreign sun.

An Internet café
where I'm trying to sculpt your absence.
Separating us, the gray casino
on this shore Ovid once paced in exile,
where money now makes love to death.

And the house where my Uncle Livius
used to read me poems: Homer,
Blaga, Cavafy.

At Day's End, the Miracle

I wash, iron, write.
Then wash again, iron, write again.
Every morning I feed the doves
and listen to more and more disturbing news.
I watch all the people around me
speeding in jeeps and airplanes.
But I also consider the leaf
in its lazy descent
while I hang wash on the clothesline.
I take time to examine the yellow rose
that snagged my busy dress.

It's my hope never to judge
my fellow creatures
with the quick scorn that met
the ragged monk, sheathed
in the ice of his long journey,
returning at last to his small village
in the Balkans.

In an unlit room he was praying
for his fellow villagers' sins
when a beam of light
streaked across the dark, walled space.
The monk pulled the frayed sweater
from over his patched black cassock,
and hung it on the sunbeam to dry.

Circles and Circles

The circle of roses in the park
hidden deep in the shadow of apartment towers
is nothing like the moon-cool circle of milk
carried in the pitcher by the nun's hands,
splashing its slow light on the grassy path—or
the sweet circle of honey that swerves before dawn
inside the bear stalked by hunters
while dew and mist beat the forest's staccato call to prayer
on the *toaca*.

The circle of wild strawberries I offered,
incapable of healing
the dark circles under my mother's eyes
during her last summer.

Or the mirror of the iron band
girdling the old oak tree,
attracting clouds, hours, seconds—
that steady, gentle flow of the day's tide.

A streak of lightning
and all the circles break open.
Thunder, and they contract,
then merge into one, burning
on the surrendered hand
like a ring of fire around fire.

On the Seashore

A plate of grapes,
a slice of fresh bread
and my consciousness
of unrepeatable joy
beside the emerald
of the sea.

And in exactly these things
God the jeweler
finds rest.

Poem with a Blue Door

I walk through the snow in blue sandals.
My red heels shiver
as when I used to run barefoot in childhood
through the blue grass of the Orăștie Mountains.

I'd play with a mirror
until the arrow of a sun ray pierced
my mother's perfumed palm
while her hand ran the comb
through my hair,
more blond each morning.

At night, its cousin, a moon ray,
luminous arrow, would stop the years
on the threshold of my house in Sibiu.

Through the blue door of this poem
I glimpse the sea,
           a basket of sour cherries,
                    and my father facing the sea
                             in a white shirt, still young,
                                      writing something.
                                           A letter.

Dream in the River's Mouth

Surrounded by an island of stones and grass,
I was dreaming in the river's mouth
when a horse, led by an old peasant,
lowered its head
to quench its thirst.

I was dreaming in the river's mouth
here at the foot of a blue mountain
stabbed high into the evening's last word.

Oh, the light of the old man's smile
when he asked me to hold his horse
so he too could drink the crystalline water!
I trembled at the life force
that surged in the young animal's body,
my hand at the bridle,
hardly daring to move next to
such poised beauty.

Bees encircled us with the balm of their buzzing,
small nuggets of gold embroidery glinting into
my solitude in the mountains.

Suddenly this landscape
slips to another: narrow lanes, houses
peeking from behind other houses
cascading to the sea.
Ah, Lisbon, city with a thousand lives.
Yellow trolleys climb steep hills.
The town fans out at my feet
and from high above, I see the brown despair
of the old cafe where Pessoa

used to sip espresso, or absinthe.

A wind like a gust of joy
envelops me
the moment I kneel
in the church of Saint Anthony
under the sky of his childhood,
where he dashed through streets rich with spices,
past palaces wreathed by orange groves
toward the *Mar de palha*, a sparkling bay
bright with spinnakers.

And how strong the temptation
must have been, almost irresistible—
how great the boy's power
when, with his finger, young Anthony
dug the sign of the cross
into the stone of the church.

Dreaming in the river's mouth,
I return home to my island
of stones and grass, the sweet
spring grass of lambs.

Notes

It's Not a Good Time for Poets *(page 18)*: The city of *Sibiu*, where Liliana Ursu was born, is nestled in a depression amid a number of mountain ranges; it has long been a focal point of Romanian culture. Historically, Sibiu was an important center in the Principality of Transylvania, for a time its capital. The *Cibin market* is in the lower town, along the Cibin River that runs through the city.

Winter Scene with My Parents' House *(page 31)*: *Cotroceni* is a still elegant district to the west of central Bucharest, mostly constructed between the two World Wars. It's where Ursu lives in a house with a small garden behind it. The *Boulevard of Heroes* is the main thoroughfare through the district. The *Samurcași Monastery* is one of a number of monasteries near Bucharest. *Waring Avenue* in State College, PA, is the street Ursu lived on during her second Fulbright stay at Penn State, 1997-98; other references to State College appear in poems on later pages: *Mount Nittany*, and *Pugh*, *Garner*, and *Allen Streets*.

Scene from Apold de Jos *(page 34)*: *Apold de Jos* ("Lower Apold") and *Saliște* are among the many rural villages in the mountainous region surrounding Sibiu.

Square of the Ravens *(page 44)*: *Corbeni Square* means the *Square of the Ravens*. The relics of the thirteenth-century *St. Dimitri*—Saint Dimitri(e) Basarabov, also called Saint Dimitri(e) the New—are deposited in the Patriarchal Cathedral in Bucharest; he is celebrated by Romanians on October 27. *Medjugorje* is a town in Bosnia and Herzegovina where the Virgin Mary was reported to have appeared to a half dozen witnesses in 1981. The Romanian poet *Tradem—*

penname of Traian Demetrescu (1866-1896)—was saluted by the Romanian master George Bacovia (1881-1957) in a line that spoke of "the ravens of the poet Tradem."

To Father Cleopa *(page 49)*: The monk *Cleopa* (1912-98) became a renowned holy man of the Romanian Orthodox Church. He resisted communist pressure by living for a dozen years as a hermit in the forest, later to return to his monastery of Sihastria, where many flocked to hear his teaching. The *toaca* is a wooden board, curved when fixed between supports, straight when meant to be carried. It is beaten in rhythmic patterns with a small mallet as a call to prayer. Some are also made of iron.

Pilgrimage to Outeiro *(page 50)*: *Outeiro* is a town in Portugal. The martyr *Saint Quintino* (Quentin) was tortured and killed by decapitation in 287 A.D.

Scene with Wash on a Clothesline *(page 53)*: *Sighet*, or Sighetu Marmației, is very close to the border with Ukraine in Romania's north; the city was the site of one of Romania's most notorious political prisons, where members of political and religious elites were incarcerated after the imposition of the communist state in 1948. Former Soviet prisoners were repatriated to Romania through Sighet Prison. Now it has become a museum, part of the Memorial to the Victims of Communism and the Resistance.

To Mother Alexandra *(page 57)*: The *Orthodox Monastery of the Transfiguration*, a monastery for women in western Pennsylvania, was founded in 1967 by *Mother Alexandra*, the former Princess Ileana of Romania.

A Visit to Peleș Castle, Seen from Pennsylvania *(page 64)*: The ornate *Peleș Castle*, originally built as a royal residence in the late 19th and early 20th centuries, does contain a room decorated by the young Gustav *Klimt*. Peleș is located at the edge of the mountain resort of

Sinaia between Bucharest and the city of Brașov. *Helen Dunmore* is the prize-winning British poet and fiction writer; *Mircea Ivănescu* (born 1931) is a major Romanian poet of the last third of the 20th century; he still lives in the city of Sibiu.

For Ann, on Her Birthday *(page 72)*: The *red eggs* are closely linked to Easter in Orthodox countries, the red color signifying Christ's blood.

Eating Grapes in February *(page 90)* and **Longing for the Sea** *(page 98)*: The traditional Romanian dish, *mămăligă*, is a mixture of yellow cornmeal, salt, and water, boiled in a cast-iron pot until thick and then turned out like a loaf on a board or table. It was often used as a substitute for bread. Western cuisine knows it as *polenta*.

Poem with a White Feather and Two Streets *(page 93)*: *Saint Stephen Street* in Bucharest is where Ursu lived with her parents for two years as a young child; *Steven Street* is close to where she lived in Louisville, KY, when Ursu was visiting professor at the University of Louisville in the spring of 2000.

The Perfect Street *(page 94)*: This poem was inspired by Steven Street in Louisville, which is near Bardstown Road and not far from *Cherokee Road. Calea Victoriei*—the Avenue of Victory—is a major thoroughfare in Bucharest, once Bucharest's grandest street, especially between World War I and II.

Room 411 *(page 97)*: This was Liliana Ursu's office number in Burrowes Building on the Penn State University Park campus during her second Fulbright residency.

The Sand of Olimp *(page 101)*: *Olimp* (Olympus) is one of a string of Romanian Black Sea resorts, many of which have names from the Greek pantheon. The poet *George Szirtes*, who came to Britain in 1956 as a refugee, has become a major voice in English poetry, and he is an important translator from Hungarian.

The Night Comes Riding *(page 102)*: *Enkidu*, the wild man, becomes the close male companion of the hero in the epic *Gilgamesh*. Enkidu is civilized through his seduction by a temple concubine.

Sfumato *(page 104)*: The Italian title, *sfumato*, means "smoky" or "gone in smoke."

Photographs of Gabriela Mistral *(page 106)*: The Chilean poet *Gabriela Mistral* won the Nobel Prize in Literature in 1945.

Love Song *(page 107)*: *Un chevalier de la bonne espérance*—a knight of good hope.

Requiem for a Wasp *(page 114)*: The streets named are in Bucharest.

The Poet

Liliana Ursu, award-winning and internationally acclaimed Romanian poet, was born in the city of Sibiu, which figures prominently in many of her eight volumes of poetry. *A Path to the Sea*, new poems translated by Ursu, Adam J. Sorkin, and Tess Gallagher, brings together poems from the poet's birthplace, her sojourns in the United States, and her adopted city of Bucharest, where she still lives. There, for over a quarter of a century, she produced and presented an acclaimed weekly literary program on Romanian National Radio, which featured interviews, poetry, and book reviews, with special focus on contemporary world poetry. Ursu has twice been Fulbright Lecturer at Penn State University. She has served as visiting professor of creative writing at the University of Louisville and Poet-in-Residence at the Stadler Center, Bucknell University. She has also taught as a visiting faculty member at the University of Bucharest.

Her first collection in English, *The Sky Behind the Forest* (Bloodaxe, 1997), translated by Ursu, Sorkin, and Gallagher, became a British Poetry Book Society "Recommended Translation" and was short-listed for the Oxford Weidenfeld Prize. Sean Cotter translated *Goldsmith Market* (Zephyr, 2003) and *Lightwall* (Zephyr, 2009), the latter a finalist for the PEN USA 2010 Literary Award in Translation. Translations of Ursu with Bruce Weigl came out in *Angel Riding a Beast* (Northwestern, 1998). Her poems also appear widely in various European languages, notably a book-length selection in German in Zurich in 2005. In addition, Ursu has written two books of short fiction and has produced ten books of translation.

Liliana Ursu's literary achievement has been praised as "a true joy for readers" by Nina Cassian. Further, Cassian remarks that Ursu's poetic imagination offers "freshness, frankness, analyzed emotions, colorful ideas – all leading to and making heard the pure sound of poetry."

This sensual, richly resonant and spiritual poetry defines why Liliana Ursu's reputation in her native country has won her major recognitions, including prizes in Romania for poetry and translation from the Romanian Writers' Union and Romania's highest national cultural honor: the rank of Knight of Arts and Literature. She is welcomed worldwide at poetry conferences and festivals as one of Europe's outstanding poets.

The Translators

Tess Gallagher's *Midnight Lantern: New and Selected Poems* will be published Fall 2011 from Graywolf Press. *The Sky Behind the Forest* was the first book by Liliana Ursu which Ms. Gallagher worked on with the poet and Adam Sorkin. Gallagher is the author of eight volumes of poetry, including *Dear Ghosts, Moon Crossing Bridge*, and *Amplitude*. Her *The Man from Kinvara: Selected Stories* was published in fall 2009. In 2008 Blackstaff Press in Belfast published *Barnacle Soup—Stories from the West of Ireland*, a collaboration with the Irish storyteller Josie Gray. *Distant Rain*, a conversation with the highly respected Buddhist nun, Jacucho Setouchi, of Kyoto, is both an art book and a cross cultural moment. Gallagher is also the author of *Amplitude, Soul Barnacles: Ten More Years with Ray, A Concert of Tenses: Essays on Poetry*, and two collections of short fiction: *At the Owl Woman Saloon* and *The Lover of Horses and Other Stories*. She has also spearheaded the publication of Raymond Carver's *Beginners* in Library of America's *Collected Stories by Raymond Carver* published Fall 2009. Jonathan Cape published Carver's *Beginners* as a single volume in the UK, also in fall 2009. She spends time in a cottage on Lough Arrow in Co. Sligo in the West of Ireland and also lives and writes in her hometown of Port Angeles, Washington. She teaches each winter term at the Northwest Institute of Literary Arts in its MFA Program on Whidby Island.

Adam J. Sorkin has translated more than forty books of contemporary Romanian literature. His recent books include two collections from the University of Plymouth Press (U.K.), Ioan Es. Pop's *No Way Out of Hadesburg* (2010) and Mircea Ivănescu's *lines poems poetry* (2009), both translated with Lidia Vianu, and he is the main translator of Carmen Firan's *Rock and Dew* (Sheep

Meadow Press, 2010), in collaboration with Firan. In 2009, he published *Memory Glyphs: Three Prose Poets from Romania* (Twisted Spoon Press), and in 2008, Ruxandra Cesereanu's *Crusader-Woman*, translated with Cesereanu (Black Widow Press). With Vianu, he was awarded the Poetry Translation Prize of the Poetry Society (U.K.) for Marin Sorescu's *The Bridge* (Bloodaxe Books, 2004), and his prior Bloodaxe Books, Liliana Ursu's *The Sky Behind the Forest* (1997), translated with Ursu and Tess Gallagher, and Ioana Ieronim's *The Triumph of the Water Witch* (2000), translated with Ieronim, were both short-listed for the Oxford Weidenfeld Prize. Sorkin's work has won the *International Quarterly* Crossing Boundaries Award and the Kenneth Rexroth Memorial Translation Prize, as well as National Endowment for the Arts, Rockefeller Foundation, Academy of American Poets, Arts Council of England, Fulbright, and Witter Bynner Foundation support. Forthcoming is an anthology of contemporary Romanian poets of the 1990s and 2000s, *The Vanishing Point That Whistles* (Talisman House). He is Distinguished Professor of English, Penn State Brandywine.

Poetry Books from Pleasure Boat Studio: A Literary Press

(Note: Empty Bowl Press is a Division of Pleasure Boat Studio.)

Songs from a Yahi Bow: Poems about Ishi • Yusef Komanyakaa, Mike O'Connor, Scott Ezell • $13.95

Beautiful Passing Lives • Ed Harkness • $15

Immortality • Mike O'Connor • $16

Painting Brooklyn • Paintings by Nina Talbot, Poetry by Esther Cohen • $20

Ghost Farm • Pamela Stewart • $13

Unknown Places • Peter Kantor, trans. from Hungarian by Michael Blumenthal • $14

Moonlight in the Redemptive Forest • Michael Daley • includes a CD • $16

Lessons Learned • Finn Wilcox • $10 • an empty bowl book

Jew's Harp • Walter Hess • $14

The Light on Our Faces • Lee Whitman-Raymond • $13

Petroglyph Americana • Scott Ezell • $15 • an empty bowl book

God Is a Tree, and Other Middle-Age Prayers • Esther Cohen • $10

Home & Away: The Old Town Poems • Kevin Miller • $15

Old Tale Road • Andrew Schelling • $15 • an empty bowl book

Working the Woods, Working the Sea • Eds. Finn Wilcox, Jerry Gorsline • $22 • an empty bowl book

The Blossoms Are Ghosts at the Wedding • Tom Jay • with essays • $15 • an empty bowl book

Against Romance • Michael Blumenthal • $14

Days We Would Rather Know • Michael Blumenthal • $14

Craving Water • Mary Lou Sanelli • $15

When the Tiger Weeps • Mike O'Connor • with prose • 15

Concentricity • Sheila E. Murphy • $13.95

The Immigrant's Table • Mary Lou Sanelli • with recipes • $14

Women in the Garden • Mary Lou Sanelli • $14

Saying the Necessary • Edward Harkness • $14

Nature Lovers • Charles Potts • $10

The Politics of My Heart • William Slaughter • $13

The Rape Poems • Frances Driscoll • $13

Our Chapbook Series:

No. 1: *The Handful of Seeds: Three and a Half Essays* • Andrew Schelling • $7 • nonfiction

No. 2: *Original Sin* • Michael Daley • $8

No. 3: *Too Small to Hold You* • Kate Reavey • $8

No. 4: *The Light on Our Faces* – re-issued in non-chapbook (see above list)

No. 5: Eye • *William Bridges* • $8

No. 6: *Selected New Poems of Rainer Maria Rilke* • trans. fm German by Alice Derry • $10
No. 7: *Through High Still Air: A Season at Sourdough Mountain* • Tim McNulty • $9 • with prose
No. 8: *Sight Progress* • Zhang Er, trans. fm Chinese by Rachel Levitsky • $9 • prosepoems
No. 9: *The Perfect Hour* • Blas Falconer • $9
No. 10: *Fervor* • Zaedryn Meade • $10
No. 11: *Some Ducks* • Tim McNulty • $10
No. 12: *Late August* • Barbara Brackney • $10
No. 13: *The Right to Live Poetically* • Emily Haines • $9

From other publishers (in limited editions):

Desire • Jody Aliesan • $14 • an empty bowl book
Deams of the Hand • Susan Goldwitz • $14 • an empty bowl book
The Basin: Poems from a Chinese Province • Mike O'Connor • $10 / $20 • an empty bowl book (paper/ hardbound)
The Straits • Michael Daley • $10 • an empty bowl book
In Our Hearts and Minds: The Northwest and Central America • Ed. Michael Daley • $12 • with prose • an empty bowl book
The Rainshadow • Mike O'Connor • $16 • an empty bowl book
Untold Stories • William Slaughter • $10 / $20 • an empty bowl book (paper / hardbound)
In Blue Mountain Dusk • Tim McNulty • $12.95 • an empty bowl book
China Basin • Clemens Starck • $13.95 • a Story Line Press book
Journeyman's Wages • Clemens Starck • $10.95 • a Story Line Press book

Orders: Pleasure Boat Studio books are available by order from your bookstore, directly from our website, or through the following:
SPD (Small Press Distribution) Tel. 8008697553, Fax 5105240852
Partners/West Tel. 4252278486, Fax 4252042448
Baker & Taylor 8007751100, Fax 8007757480
Ingram Tel 6157935000, Fax 6152875429
Amazon.com or **Barnesandnoble.com**

Pleasure Boat Studio: A Literary Press
201 West 89th Street
New York, NY 10024
Tel / Fax: 8888105308
www.pleasureboatstudio.com / pleasboat@nyc.rr.com